Renal Diet Cookbook for Beginners 2021

The Complete Science-Backed Recipe Book for Long Lasting Health

Lillie Melton

CONTENTS

BREAKFAST

Eggplant Fries

Prep Time: 15 minutes

Cook Time: 10 minutes

Yeld: 8

Ingredients:

- 2 eggs
- 2 cups almond flour
- 2 tablespoons coconut oil, spray
- 2 eggplants, peeled and cut thinly
- Salt and pepper

Steps:

1. Preheat your oven to 400 °F
2. Take a bowl and mix with salt and black pepper in it
3. Take another bowl and beat eggs until frothy
4. Dip the eggplant pieces into the eggs
5. Then coat them with the flour mixture
6. Add another layer of flour and egg
7. Then, take a baking sheet and grease with coconut oil on top
8. Bake for about 15 minutes

Per Serving: Calories: 212 Fat: 15.8g Carbohydrates: 12.1g Protein: 8.6g

Pineapple Oatmeal

Prep Time: 10 minutes

Cook Time: 4-8 hours

Yeld: 5

Ingredients:

- 1 cup steel-cut oats
- 4 cups unsweetened almond almond milk
- 2 medium apples, slashed
- 1 teaspoon coconut oil
- 1 teaspoon cinnamon
- ¼ teaspoon nutmeg
- 2 tablespoons maple syrup, unsweetened
- A drizzle of lemon juice

Steps:

1. Add the listed ingredients to a cooking pan and mix well
2. Cook on a very low flame for 8 hours or on high flame for 4 hours
3. Gently stir
4. Add your desired toppings
5. Stock in the fridge for later use, make sure to add a splash of almond almond milk after re-heating for added flavor

Per Serving: Calories: 180 Fat: 5g Carbohydrates: 31g Protein: 5g

Simple Chia Porridge

Prep Time: 10 minutes

Cook Time: 5-10 minutes

Yeld: 2

Ingredients:

- 1 tablespoon chia seeds
- 1 tablespoon ground flaxseed
- 1/3 cup coconut cream
- ½ cup of water
- 1 teaspoon vanilla extract
- 1 tablespoon almond butter

Steps:

1. Add chia seeds, coconut cream, flaxseed, water and vanilla to a small pot
2. Mix and let it sit for 7 minutes
3. Put almond butter and place pot over low heat
4. Keep stirring as almond butter melts
5. Once the porridge is hot/not boiling, pour into a bowl
6. Add a few berries or a dash of cream for extra flavor

Per Serving: Calories: 410 Fat: 38g Carbohydrates: 10g Protein: 6g

Pepperoni Omelet

Prep Time: 5 minutes

Cook Time: 20 minutes

Yeld: 2

Ingredients:

- 3 eggs
- 7 pepperoni slices
- 1 teaspoon coconut cream
- Salt and ground black pepper, to taste
- 2 tablespoon almond butter

Steps:

1. Take a bowl and whisk eggs with all the remaining ingredients
2. Then take a skillet and heat the butter
3. Pour one quarter of the egg mixture into your skillet
4. After that, cook for 2 minutes per side
5. Repeat to use the entire batter

Per Serving: Calories: 141 Fat: 11.5g Carbohydrates: 0.6g Protein: 8.9g

Scrambled Turkey Eggs

Prep Time: 15 minutes

Cook Time: 15 minutes

Yeld: 2

Ingredients:

- 1 tablespoon coconut oil
- 1 medium red bell pepper, diced
- ½ medium yellow onion, diced
- ¼ teaspoon hot pepper sauce
- 3 large free-range eggs
- ¼ teaspoon black pepper, freshly ground
- ¼ teaspoon salt

Steps:

1. Put a pan to medium-high heat and add coconut oil, let it heat up
2. Add onions and Saute
3. Add turkey and red pepper
4. Cook until turkey is cooked
5. Take a bowl and beat eggs, stir in salt and pepper
6. Pour eggs in the pan with turkey and gently cook and scramble eggs
7. Top with hot sauce and enjoy!

Per Serving: Calories: 435 Fat: 30g Carbohydrates: 34g Protein: 16g

Cinnamon Flavored Baked Apple Chips

Prep Time: 5 minutes

Cook Time: 2 hours

Yeld: 2

Ingredients:

- 1 teaspoon cinnamon

- 1-2 apples

Steps:

1. Preheat your oven to 200 °F
2. Take a sharp knife and slice apples into thin slices
3. Discard seeds
4. Make sure they do not overlap
5. Once done, sprinkle cinnamon over the apples
6. Bake in the oven for 1 hour
7. Flip and bake for an hour more until no longer moist

Per Serving: Calories: 147 Fat: 0g Carbohydrates: 39g Protein: 1g

Apple & Cinnamon French Toast

Prep Time: 20 minutes

Cook Time: 50 minutes

Yeld: 12

Ingredients:

- Cooking spray
- 1 lb. loaf cinnamon raisin bread, cubed
- 1 apple, diced
- 6 tablespoons butter
- 1 teaspoon ground cinnamon
- 8 eggs
- 1 cup half and half
- ¼ cup pancake syrup
- 1 cup almond almond milk

Steps:

1. Spray oil on a baking dish.
2. Arrange half of the bread cubes
3. Top with the apples.
4. Sprinkle the cinnamon over the apple and bread.
5. Top with the remaining bread cubes.
6. In a bowl, beat eggs with half and half.
7. Add syrup, almond almond milk and butter.
8. Pour mixture over the bread.
9. Cover with foil.
10. Refrigerate for 2 hours.

11. Let cool for 10 minutes before serving.

12. Slice into 12 Yeld.

Per Serving: Calories 324 Protein 9 g Carbohydrates 27 g Fat 20 g Cholesterol 170 mg Sodium 280 mg Potassium 224 mg Phosphorus 150 mg Fiber 1.8 g

Blueberry Smoothie in a Bowl

Prep Time: 15 minutes

Cook Time: 0 minutes

Serving: 1

Ingredients:

- 1 cup frozen blueberries
- 1/4 cup plain Greek yogurt
- 2 tablespoons whey protein powder
- 1/4 cup vanilla almond almond milk (unsweetened)
- 1 tablespoon cereal
- 5 raspberries, sliced
- 2 strawberries, sliced
- 2 teaspoons coconut flakes

Steps:

1. Put the blueberries, yogurt, whey protein powder and almond almond milk in a blender.

2. Blend until smooth.

3. Pour mixture into a bowl.

4. Top with cereal, raspberries and strawberries.

5. Sprinkle coconut flakes on top.

Per Serving: Calories 225 Protein 17 g Carbohydrates 28 g Fat 5 g Cholesterol 3 mg Sodium 118 mg Potassium 370 mg Phosphorus 174 mg Calcium 240 mg Fiber 7.8 g

Egg Pockets

Prep Time: 15 minutes

Cook Time: 20 minutes

Yeld: 4

Ingredients:

- 1 teaspoon dry yeast
- 1 cup warm water
- 1 tablespoon oil
- 1 teaspoon garlic powder
- 2 cups all-purpose flour
- 1 tablespoon sugar
- 3 eggs, beat
- Cooking spray

Steps:

1. Dissolve the yeast in water.
2. Add the oil, garlic powder, flour and sugar.
3. Form soft dough from the mixture.
4. Let it sit for 5 minutes.
5. Roll out the dough and slice into 4 portions.
6. Create a bowl with the dough.
7. Beat the eggs.
8. Put egg on top of the dough.

9. Fold the dough and pinch the edges.

10. Bake in the oven at 350 degrees F for 20 minutes.

Per Serving: Calories 321 Protein 11 g Carbohydrates 25 g Fat 7 g Cholesterol 123 mg Sodium 50 mg Potassium 139 mg Phosphorus 130 mg Calcium 30 mg Fiber 2 g

Italian Eggs with Peppers

Prep Time: 15 minutes

Cook Time: 20 minutes

Yeld: 6

Ingredients:

- 1/2 cup onion, minced
- 1 cup red bell pepper, chopped
- 8 eggs, beaten
- Black pepper to taste
- 1/4 cup fresh basil, chopped

Steps:

1. In a skillet, cook onion and red bell pepper until soft.
2. Season eggs with black pepper.
3. Pour egg mixture into the pan.
4. Cook without mixing until firm.
5. Sprinkle fresh basil on top before serving.

Per Serving: Calories 194 Protein 13 g Carbohydrates 5 g Fat 14 g Cholesterol 423 mg Sodium 141 mg Potassium 222 mg Phosphorus 203 mg Calcium 64 mg Fiber 0.8 g

Mushroom Omelet

Prep Time: 10 minutes

Cook Time: 5 minutes

Yeld: 2

Ingredients:

- 2 teaspoons butter
- 2 tablespoons onion, chopped
- 1/2 cup mushroom, diced
- 1/4 cup sweet red peppers, chopped
- 3 eggs, beaten
- 1 teaspoon Worcestershire sauce
- 1/4 teaspoon black pepper

Steps:

1. Melt butter in a pan over medium heat.
2. Cook the onion, mushroom and sweet peppers for 5 minutes.
3. Remove from the pan and set aside.
4. Mix the eggs and Worcestershire sauce.
5. Cook eggs over medium heat.
6. When the edges start to become firm, add onion mixture on top.
7. Season with pepper.
8. Fold the omelet.

Per Serving: Calories 199 Protein 11 g Carbohydrates 4 g Fat 15 g Cholesterol 341 mg Sodium 276 mg Potassium 228 mg Phosphorus 167 mg Calcium 55 mg Fiber 0.6 g

Asparagus Frittata

Prep Time: 5 minutes

Cook Time: 30 minutes

Yeld: 2 Yeld

Ingredients:

- 10 medium asparagus spears, ends trimmed
- 2 teaspoons extra-virgin olive oil, divided
- Freshly ground black pepper
- 4 large eggs
- ½ teaspoon onion powder
- ¼ cup chopped parsley

Steps:

1. heat the oven to 350°F.

2. Mix the asparagus with 1 teaspoon of olive oil and season with pepper. Place to a baking pan and roast, stirring occasionally, for 20 minutes, until the spears are browned and tender.

3. In a small bowl, beat the eggs with the onion powder and parsley. Season with pepper.

4. Cut the asparagus spears into 1-inch pieces and arrange in a medium skillet. Drizzle with the remaining oil, and shake the pan to distribute.

5. Pour the egg mixture into the skillet, and cook over medium heat. When the egg is well set on the bottom and nearly set on the top, cover it with a plate, invert the pan so the frittata is on the plate, and then slide it back into the pan with the cooked-side up. Continue to cook for about 30 more seconds, until firm.

Per Serving: Calories: 102; Total Fat: 8g; Saturated Fat: 2g; Cholesterol: 104mg; Carbohydrates: 4g; Fiber: 2g; Protein: 6g; Phosphorus: 103mg; Potassium: 248mg; Sodium: 46mg

Poached Eggs with Cilantro Butter

Prep Time: 5 minutes

Cook Time: 10 minutes

Yield: 2 Yeld

Ingredients:

- 2 tablespoons unsalted butter
- 1 tablespoon chopped parsley
- 1 tablespoon chopped cilantro
- 4 large eggs
- Dash vinegar
- Freshly ground black pepper

Steps:

1. In a small pan over low heat, melt the butter. Add the parsley and cilantro, and cook for about 1 minute, stirring constantly. Remove from the heat, and pour into a small dish.

2. In a small saucepan, bring about 3 inches of water to a simmer. Add the dash of vinegar.

3. Crack 1 egg into a cup or ramekin. Using a spoon, create a whirlpool in the simmering water, and then pour the egg into the water. Use the spoon to draw the white together until just starting to set. Repeat with the remaining eggs. Cook for 4 to 7 minutes, depending on how set you like your yolk.

4. With a slotted spoon, remove the eggs.

5. Serve the eggs topped with 1 tablespoon of the herbed butter and some pepper.

Per Serving: Calories: 261; Total Fat: 22g; Saturated Fat: 7g; Cholesterol: 429mg; Carbohydrates: 1g; Fiber: 0g; Protein: 14g; Phosphorus: 226mg; Potassium: 173mg; Sodium: 164mg

Chorizo and Egg Tortilla

Prep Time: 10 minutes

Cook Time: 13 minutes

Yeld: 1 tortilla

Ingredients:

- 1 flour tortilla, about 6-inches
- 1/3 cup chorizo meat, chopped
- 1 egg

Steps:

1. Take a medium-sized skillet pan, place it over medium heat and when hot, add chorizo.

2. When the meat has cooked, drain the excess fat, whisk an egg, pour it into the pan, stir until combined, and cook for 3 minutes, or until eggs have cooked.

3. Spoon egg onto the tortilla and then serve.

Per Serving: Calories – 223 Fat – 11 g Protein – 16 g Carbohydrates – 15 g Fiber – 1.5 g

Cottage Pancakes

Prep Time: 10 minutes

Cook Time: 50 minutes

Yeld: 6 pancakes

Ingredients:

- 3 cups fresh raspberries, sliced
- ½ cup all-purpose white flour
- 6 tablespoons unsalted butter, melted
- 4 eggs, beaten

Steps:

1. Crack eggs in a medium-sized bowl, add flour, and butter in it, and whisk until combined.

2. Take a medium-high frying pan, grease it with oil and when hot, pour in prepared batter, ¼ cup of batter per pancake, spread the batter into a 4-inch pancake, and cook for 3 minutes per side until browned.

3. When done, transfer pancakes onto a plate, cook more pancakes in the same manner, and, when done, serve each pancake with ½ sliced raspberries.

Per Serving: Calories – 253 Fat – 17 g Protein – 11 g

Carbohydrates – 21 g Fiber – 2 g

Egg in a Hole

Prep Time: 5 minutes

Cook Time: 5 minutes

Yeld: 1 slice

Ingredients:

- 1 slice of white bread
- ¼ teaspoon lemon pepper seasoning, salt-free

- 1 egg

Steps:

1. Prepare the bread by making a hole in the middle: use a cookie cutter for cutting out the center.

2. Brush the slice with oil on both sides, then take a medium-sized skillet pan, place it over medium heat and when hot, add bread slice in it, crack the egg in the center of the slice sprinkle with lemon pepper seasoning.

3. Cook the egg for 2 minutes, then carefully flip it along with the slice and continue cooking for an additional 2 minutes.

Per Serving: Calories – 159 Fat – 7 g Protein – 9 g Carbohydrates – 15 g Fiber – 0.8 g

German Pancakes

Prep Time: 10 minutes

Cook Time: 15 minutes

Yeld: 10 pancakes

Ingredients:

- 2/3 cup all-purpose flour
- ¼ teaspoon vanilla extract, unsweetened
- 2 tablespoons white sugar
- 1 cup almond milk, low-fat
- 4 eggs
- 1/3 cup fruit jam for serving, sugar-free

Steps:

1. Prepare the batter by taking a medium-sized bowl, add flour in it along with sugar, stir until mixed, whisk in eggs until blended, and then whisk in vanilla and almond milk until smooth.

2. Take a skillet pan, about 8 inches, spray it with oil and when hot, add 3 tablespoons of the prepared batter, tilt the pan to spread the batter evenly

3. Flip the pancake, continue cooking for 45 seconds until the other side is browned, and when done, transfer pancake to a plate.

4. Cook nine more pancakes in the same manner and, when done on one side of the pancake, fold it, and then serve with 1 tablespoon of fruit jam.

Per Serving: Calories – 74 Fat – 2 g Protein – 4 g Carbohydrates – 10 g Fiber – 0.2 g

Mushroom and Red Pepper Omelet

Prep Time: 5 minutes

Cook Time: 12 minutes

Yeld: 2 plates

Ingredients:

- 2 tablespoons white onion, diced
- ¼ cup sweet red peppers, diced
- ½ cup mushrooms, diced
- ¼ teaspoon ground black pepper
- 1 teaspoon Worcestershire sauce
- 2 teaspoons unsalted butter
- 3 eggs

Steps:

1. Take a medium-sized skillet pan, place it over medium heat, add 1 teaspoon butter until onions are tender.

2. Stir in red pepper, then transfer vegetables to a plate and set aside until needed.

3. Crack the eggs in a bowl, add Worcestershire sauce, and whisk until combined.

4. Return skillet pan over medium heat, add remaining butter and when it melts, pour in the egg mixture, and cook for 2 minutes, or until omelet is partially cooked.

5. Then top cooked vegetables on one side of the omelet, and continue cooking until omelet is cooked completely.

6. When done, remove the pan from the heat, cover the omelet's filling by folding the other half of the omelet, sprinkle it with black pepper, and then divide omelet into two.

7. Serve straight away.

Per Serving: Calories – 199 Fat – 15 g Protein – 11 g Carbohydrates – 4 g Fiber – 0.6 g

Curried Cauliflower

Prep Time: 5 minutes

Cook Time: 20 minutes

Yeld: 4 Yeld

Ingredients:

- 1 tsp. turmeric
- 1 diced onion
- 1 tbsp. chopped fresh cilantro
- 1 tsp. cumin
- ½ diced chili
- ½ cup water
- 1 minced garlic clove
- 1 tbsp. coconut oil
- 1 tsp. garam masala
- 2 cups cauliflower florets

Steps:

1. Add the oil to a skillet on medium heat.
2. Sauté the onion and garlic for 5 minutes until soft.
3. Add the cumin, turmeric and garam masala and stir to release the aromas.
4. Now add the chili to the pan along with the cauliflower.
5. Stir to coat.
6. Pour in the water and reduce the heat to a simmer for 15 minutes.
7. Garnish with cilantro to serve.

Per Serving: Calories: 108 kcal; Total Fat: 7 g; Saturated Fat: 0 g; Cholesterol: 0 mg; Sodium: 35 mg; Total Carbs: 11 g; Fiber: 0 g; Sugar: 0 g; Protein: 2 g

Chinese Tempeh Stir Fry

Prep Time: 5 minutes

Cook Time: 15 minutes

Yeld: 2 Yeld

Ingredients:

- 2 oz. sliced tempeh
- 1 cup cooked rice
- 1 minced garlic clove
- ½ cup green onions
- 1 tsp. minced fresh ginger
- 1 tbsp. coconut oil
- ½ cup corn

Steps:

1. Heat the oil in a skillet or wok on a high heat and add the garlic and ginger.
2. Sauté for 1 minute.
3. Now add the tempeh and cook for 5-6 minutes before adding the corn for a further 10 minutes.
4. Now add the green onions and serve over rice.

Per Serving: Calories: 304 kcal; Total Fat: 4 g; Saturated Fat: 0 g; Cholesterol: 0 mg; Sodium: 91 mg; Total Carbs: 35 g; Fiber: 0 g; Sugar: 0 g; Protein: 10 g

Egg White Frittata with Penne

Prep Time: 15 minutes

Cook Time: 30 minutes

Yeld: 4 Yeld

Ingredients:

- Egg whites- 6
- Rice almond milk – ¼ cup
- Chopped fresh parsley – 1 tbsp.
- Chopped fresh thyme – 1 tsp
- Chopped fresh chives – 1 tsp
- Ground black pepper
- Olive oil – 2 tsp.
- Small sweet onion – ¼, chopped
- Minced garlic – 1 tsp
- Boiled and chopped red bell pepper – ½ cup
- Cooked penne – 2 cups

Steps:

1. Preheat the oven to 350f.
2. In a bowl, whisk together the egg whites, rice almond milk, parsley, thyme, chives, and pepper.
3. Heat the oil in a skillet.
4. Sauté the onion, garlic, red pepper for 4 minutes or until they are softened.
5. Add the cooked penne to the skillet.
6. Pour the egg mixture over the pasta and shake the pan to coat the pasta.

7. Leave the skillet on the heat for 1 minute to set the frittata's bottom and then transfer the skillet to the oven.

8. Bake the frittata for 25 minutes, or until it is set and golden brown.

9. Serve.

Per Serving: Calories: 170 kcal; Total Fat: 3 g; Saturated Fat: 0 g; Cholesterol: 0 mg; Sodium: 90 mg; Total Carbs: 25 g; Fiber: 0 g; Sugar: 0 g; Protein: 10 g

Vegetable Fried Rice

Prep Time: 20 minutes

Cook Time: 20 minutes

Yeld: 6 Yeld

Ingredients:

- Olive oil – 1 tbsp.
- Sweet onion – ½, chopped
- Grated fresh ginger – 1 tbsp.
- Minced garlic - 2 tsp
- Sliced carrots – 1 cup
- Chopped eggplant – ½ cup
- Peas – ½ cup
- Green beans – ½ cup, cut into 1-inch pieces
- Chopped fresh cilantro – 2 tbsp.
- Cooked rice – 3 cups

Steps:

1. Heat the olive oil in a skillet.
2. Sauté the ginger, onion, and garlic for 3 minutes or until softened.
3. Stir in carrot, eggplant, green beans, and peas and sauté for 3 minutes more.
4. Add cilantro and rice.
5. Sauté, constantly stirring, for about 10 minutes or until the rice is heated through.
6. Serve.

Per Serving: Calories: 189 kcal; Total Fat: 7 g; Saturated Fat: 0 g; Cholesterol: 0 mg; Sodium: 13 mg; Total Carbs: 28 g; Fiber: 0 g; Sugar: 0 g; Protein: 6 g

Couscous Burgers

Prep Time: 20 minutes

Cook Time: 10 minutes

Yeld: 4 Yeld

Ingredients:

- chickpeas – ½ cup
- Chopped fresh cilantro – 2 tbsp.
- Chopped fresh parsley
- Lemon juice - 1 tbsp.
- Lemon zest – 2 tsp
- Minced garlic – 1 tsp
- Cooked couscous – 2 ½ cups
- Eggs – 2, lightly beaten
- Olive oil – 2 tbsp.

Steps:

1. Put the cilantro, chickpeas, parsley, lemon juice, lemon zest, and garlic in a food processor and pulse until a paste form.
2. Transfer the chickpea mixture to a bowl, and add the eggs and couscous. Mix well.
3. Chill the mixture in the refrigerator for 1 hour.
4. Form the couscous mixture into 4 patties.
5. Heat olive oil in a skillet.

6. Place the patties in the skillet, 2 at a time, gently pressing them down with the fork of a spatula.

7. Cook for 5 minutes or until golden, and flip the patties over.

8. Cook the other side for 5 minutes and transfer the cooked burgers to a plate covered with a paper towel.

9. Repeat with the remaining 2 burgers.

Per Serving: Calories: 242 kcal; Total Fat: 10 g; Saturated Fat: 0 g; Cholesterol: 0 mg; Sodium: 43 mg; Total Carbs: 29 g; Fiber: 0 g; Sugar: 0 g; Protein: 9 g

Marinated Tofu Stir-Fry

Prep Time: 20 minutes

Cook Time: 20 minutes

Yeld: 4 Yeld

Ingredients:

- For the tofu:
- Lemon juice – 1 tbsp.
- Minced garlic – 1 tsp
- Grated fresh ginger – 1 tsp
- Pinch red pepper flakes
- Extra-firm tofu- 5 ounces, pressed well and cubed
- For the stir-fry:
- Olive oil – 1 tbsp.
- Cauliflower florets – ½ cup
- Thinly sliced carrots – ½ cup
- Julienned red pepper – ½ cup
- Fresh green beans – ½ cup
- Cooked white rice – 2 cups

Steps:

1. In a bowl, mix the lemon juice, garlic, ginger, and red pepper flakes.
2. Add the tofu and toss to coat.
3. Place the bowl in the refrigerator and marinate for 2 hours.
4. To make the stir-fry, heat the oil in a skillet.

5. Sauté the tofu for 8 minutes or until it is lightly browned and heated through.

6. Add the carrots, and cauliflower and sauté for 5 minutes. Stirring and tossing constantly.

7. Add the red pepper and green beans, sauté for 3 minutes more.

8. Serve over white rice.

Per Serving: Calories: 190 kcal; Total Fat: 6 g; Saturated Fat: 0 g; Cholesterol: 0 mg; Sodium: 22 mg; Total Carbs: 30 g; Fiber: 0 g; Sugar: 0 g; Protein: 6 g

Curried Veggie Stir-Fry

Prep Time: 20 minutes

Cook Time: 10 minutes

Yeld: 6

Ingredients:

- 2 tablespoons of extra-virgin olive oil
- 1 onion, chopped
- 4 garlic cloves, minced
- 4 cups of frozen stir-fry vegetables
- 1 cup unsweetened full-fat coconut almond milk
- 1 cup of water
- 2 tablespoons of green curry paste

Steps:

1. In a wok or non-stick, heat the olive oil over medium-high heat. Stir-fry the onion and garlic for 2 to 3 minutes, until fragrant.

2. Add the frozen stir-fry vegetables and continue to cook for 3 to 4 minutes longer, or until the vegetables are hot.

3. Meanwhile, in a small bowl, combine coconut almond milk, water, and curry paste. Stir until the paste dissolves.

4. Add the broth mixture to the wok and cook for another 2 to 3 minutes, or until the sauce has reduced slightly and all the vegetables are crisp-tender.

5. Serve over couscous or hot cooked rice.

Per Serving: Calories: 293 Total fat: 18g Saturated fat: 10g Sodium: 247mg Phosphorus: 138mg Potassium: 531mg Carbohydrates: 28g Fiber: 7g Protein: 7g Sugar: 4g

Chilaquiles

Prep Time: 20 minutes

Cook Time: 20 minutes

Yeld: 4

Ingredients:

- 3 (8-inch) corn tortillas, cut into strips
- 2 tablespoons of extra-virgin olive oil
- 12 tomatillos, papery covering removed, chopped
- 3 tablespoons for freshly squeezed lime juice
- ⅛ teaspoon of salt
- ⅛ teaspoon of freshly ground black pepper
- 4 large egg whites
- 2 large eggs

- 2 tablespoons of water
- 1 cup of shredded pepper jack cheese

Steps:

1. In a dry nonstick skillet, toast the tortilla strips over medium heat until they are crisp, tossing the pan and stirring occasionally. This should take 4 to 6 minutes. Remove the strips from the pan and set aside.

2. In the same skillet, heat the olive oil over medium heat and add the tomatillos, lime juice, salt, and pepper. Cook and frequently stir for about 8 to 10 minutes until the tomatillos break down and form a sauce. Transfer the sauce to a bowl and set aside.

3. In a small bowl, beat the egg whites, eggs, and water and add to the skillet. Cook the eggs for 3 to 4 minutes, stirring occasionally until they are set and cooked to 160°F.

4. Preheat the oven to 400°F.

5. Toss the tortilla strips in the tomatillo sauce and place in a casserole dish. Top with the scrambled eggs and cheese.

6. Bake for 10 to 15 minutes, or until the cheese starts to brown. Serve.

Per Serving: Calories: 312 Total fat: 20g Saturated fat: 8g Sodium: 345mg Phosphorus: 280mg Potassium: 453mg Carbohydrates: 19g Fiber: 3g Protein: 15g Sugar: 5g

Roasted Veggie Sandwiches

Prep Time: 20 minutes

Cook Time: 35 minutes

Yield: 6

Ingredients:

- 3 bell peppers, assorted colors, sliced
- 1 cup of sliced yellow summer squash
- 1 red onion, sliced
- 2 tablespoons of extra-virgin olive oil
- 2 tablespoons of balsamic vinegar
- ⅛ teaspoon of salt
- ⅛ teaspoon of freshly ground black pepper
- 3 large whole-wheat pita breads, halved

Steps:

1. Preheat the oven to 400°F.
2. Prepare a parchment paper and line it in a rimmed baking sheet.
3. Spread the bell peppers, squash, and onion on the prepared baking sheet. Sprinkle with the olive oil, vinegar, salt, and pepper.
4. Roast for 30 to 40 minutes, turning the vegetables with a spatula once during cooking, until they are tender and light golden brown.
5. Pile the vegetables into the pita breads and serve.

Per Serving: Calories: 182 Total fat: 5g Saturated fat: 1g Sodium: 234mg Phosphorus: 106mg Potassium: 289mg Carbohydrates: 31g Fiber: 4g Protein: 5g Sugar: 6g

Pasta Fagioli

Prep Time: 25 minutes

Cook Time: 25 minutes

Yeld: 6

Ingredients:

- 1 (15-ounce) can low-sodium great northern beans, drained and rinsed, divided
- 2 cups frozen peppers and onions, thawed, divided
- 5 cups low-sodium vegetable broth
- ⅛ teaspoon salt
- ⅛ teaspoon freshly ground black pepper
- 1 cup whole-grain orecchiette pasta
- 2 tablespoons extra-virgin olive oil
- ⅓ cup grated Parmesan cheese

Steps:

1. In a large saucepan, place the beans and cover with water. Bring to a boil over high heat and boil for 10 minutes. Drain the beans.

2. In a food processor or blender, combine ⅓ cup of beans and ⅓ cup of thawed peppers and onions. Process until smooth.

3. In the same saucepan, combine the pureed mixture, the remaining 1⅔ cups of peppers and onions, the remaining beans, the broth, and the salt and pepper and bring to a simmer.

4. Add the pasta to the saucepan. Make sure to stir it and bring it to boil, reduce the heat to low, and

simmer for 8 to 10 minutes, or until the pasta is tender.

5. Serve drizzled with olive oil and topped with Parmesan cheese.

Per Serving: Calories: 245 Total fat: 7g Saturated fat: 2g Sodium: 269mg Phosphorus: 188mg Potassium: 592mg Carbohydrates: 36g Fiber: 7g Protein: 12g Sugar: 4g

Roasted Peach Open-Face Sandwich

Prep Time: 5 minutes

Cook Time: 15 minutes

Yeld: 4

Ingredients:

- 2 fresh peaches, peeled and sliced
- 1 tablespoon of extra-virgin olive oil
- 1 tablespoon of freshly squeezed lemon juice
- ⅛ teaspoon of salt
- ⅛ teaspoon of freshly ground black pepper
- 4 ounces of cream cheese, at room temperature
- 2 teaspoons of fresh thyme leaves
- 4 bread slices

Steps:

1. Preheat the oven to 400°F.

2. Arrange the peaches on a rimmed baking sheet. Brush them with olive oil on both sides.

3. Roast the peaches for 10 to 15 minutes, until they are lightly golden brown around the edges. Sprinkle with lemon juice, salt, and pepper.

4. In a small bowl, combine the cream cheese and thyme and mix well.

5. Toast the bread. Get the toasted bread and spread it with the cream cheese mixture. Top with the peaches and serve.

Per Serving: Calories: 250 Total fat: 13g Saturated fat: 6g Sodium: 376mg Phosphorus: 163mg Potassium: 260mg Carbohydrates: 28g

Fiber: 3g Protein: 6g Sugar: 8g

Spicy Corn and Rice Burritos

Prep Time: 10 minutes

Cook Time: 20 minutes

Yeld: 4

Ingredients:

- 3 tablespoons of extra-virgin olive oil, divided
- 1 (10-ounce) package of frozen cooked rice
- 1½ cups of frozen yellow corn
- 1 tablespoon of chili powder
- 1 cup of shredded pepper jack cheese
- 4 large or 6 small corn tortillas

Steps:

1. Put the skillet in over medium heat and put 2 tablespoons of olive oil. Add the rice, corn, and chili powder and cook for 4 to 6 minutes, or until the ingredients are hot.

2. Transfer the ingredients from the pan into a medium bowl. Let cool for 15 minutes.

3. Stir the cheese into the rice mixture.

4. Heat the tortillas using the Steps from the package to make them pliable. Fill the corn tortillas with the rice mixture, then roll them up.

5. At this point, you can serve them as is, or you can fry them first. Heat the remaining tablespoon of olive oil in a large skillet. Fry the burritos, seam-side down at first, turning once, until they are brown and crisp, about 4 to 6 minutes per side, then serve.

Per Serving: Calories: 386 Total fat: 21g Saturated fat: 7g Sodium: 510mg Phosphorus: 304mg Potassium: 282mg Carbohydrates: 41g Fiber: 4g Protein: 11g Sugar: 2g

Crust less Cabbage Quiche

Prep Time: 10 minutes

Cook Time: 40 minutes

Yeld: 6

Ingredients:

- Olive oil cooking spray
- 2 tablespoons of extra-virgin olive oil
- 3 cups of coleslaw blend with carrots
- 3 large eggs, beaten
- 3 large egg whites, beaten
- ½ cup of half-and-half
- 1 teaspoon of dried dill weed
- ⅛ teaspoon of salt
- ⅛ teaspoon of freshly ground black pepper

- 1 cup of grated Swiss cheese

Steps:

1. Preheat the oven to 350°F. Spray pie plate (9-inch) with cooking spray and set aside.

2. In a skillet, put an oil and put it in medium heat. Add the coleslaw mix and cook for 4 to 6 minutes, stirring, until the cabbage is tender. Transfer the vegetables from the pan to a medium bowl to cool.

3. Meanwhile, in another medium bowl, combine the eggs and egg whites, half-and-half, dill, salt, and pepper and beat to combine.

4. Stir the cabbage mixture into the egg mixture and pour into the prepared pie plate.

5. Sprinkle with the cheese.

6. Bake for 30 to 35 minutes, or until the mixture is puffed, set, and light golden brown. Let stand for 5 minutes, then slice to serve.

Per Serving: Calories: 203 Total fat: 16g Saturated fat: 6g Sodium: 321mg Phosphorus: 169mg Potassium: 155mg Carbohydrates: 5g

Fiber: 1g Protein: 11g Sugar: 4g

Vegetable Confetti

Prep Time: 25 minutes

Cook Time: 15 minutes

Yeld: 1

Ingredients:

- ½ red bell pepper
- ½ green pepper, boiled and chopped
- 4 scallions, thinly sliced
- ½ tsp. of ground cumin
- 3 tbsp. of vegetable oil
- 1 ½ tbsp. of white wine vinegar
- Black pepper to taste

Steps:

1. Join all fixings and blend well.
2. Chill in the fridge.
3. You can include a large portion of slashed jalapeno pepper for an increasingly fiery blend

Per Serving: Calories: 230 Fat: 25g Fiber: 3g Carbs: 24g Protein: 43g

Creamy Veggie Casserole

Prep Time: 25 minutes

Cook Time: 35 minutes

Yeld: 4

Ingredients:

- ⅓ cup extra-virgin olive oil, divided
- 1 onion, chopped
- 2 tablespoons flour
- 3 cups low-sodium vegetable broth
- 3 cups frozen California blend vegetables
- 1 cup crushed crisp rice cereal

Steps:

1. Preheat the oven to 375°F.
2. Next is heat 2 tablespoons of olive oil in a large skillet over medium heat. Add the onion and cook for 3 to 4 minutes, stirring, until the onion is tender.
3. Add the flour and stir for 2 minutes.
4. Add the broth to the saucepan, stirring for 3 to 4 minutes, or until the sauce starts to thicken.
5. Add the vegetables to the saucepan. Simmer and cook until vegetables are tender (for six to eight minutes).
6. When the vegetables are done, pour the mixture into a 3-quart casserole dish.
7. Sprinkle the vegetables with the crushed cereal.

8. Bake for 20 to 25 minutes or until the cereal is golden brown and the filling is bubbling. Let cool for 5 minutes and serve.

Per Serving: Calories: 234 Total fat: 18g Saturated fat: 3g Sodium: 139mg Phosphorus: 21mg Potassium: 210mg Carbohydrates: 16g

Fiber: 3g Protein: 3g Sugar: 5g

Vegetable Green Curry

Prep Time: 20 minutes

Cook Time: 20 minutes

Yield: 6

Ingredients:

- 2 tablespoons extra-virgin olive oil
- 1 head broccoli, cut into florets
- 1 bunch asparagus, cut into 2-inch lengths
- 3 tablespoons water
- 2 tablespoons green curry paste
- 1 medium eggplant
- ⅛ teaspoon salt
- ⅛ teaspoon freshly ground black pepper
- ⅔ cup plain whole-almond milk yogurt

Steps:

1. Put olive oil in a large saucepan in a medium heat. Add the broccoli and stir-fry for 5 minutes. Add the asparagus and stir-fry for another 3 minutes.

2. Meanwhile, in a small bowl, combine the water with the green curry paste.

3. Add the eggplant, curry-water mixture, salt, and pepper. Stir-fry or until vegetables are all tender.

4. Add the yogurt. Heat through but avoid simmering. Serve.

Per Serving: Calories: 113 Total fat: 6g Saturated fat: 1g Sodium: 174mg Phosphorus: 117mg Potassium: 569mg Carbohydrates: 13g

Fiber: 6g Protein: 5g Sugar: 7g

Zucchini Bowl

Prep Time: 10 minutes

Cook Time: 20 minutes

Yield: 4

Ingredients:

- 1 onion, chopped
- 3 zucchini, cut into medium chunks
- 2 tablespoons coconut almond milk
- 2 garlic cloves, minced
- 4 cups chicken stock
- 2 tablespoons coconut oil
- Pinch of salt
- Black pepper to taste

Steps:

1. Take a pot and place it over medium heat
2. Add oil and let it heat up
3. Add zucchini, garlic, onion, and stir
4. Cook for 5 minutes

5. Add stock, salt, pepper, and stir

6. Bring to a boil and lower down the heat

7. Simmer for 20 minutes.

8. Remove heat and add coconut almond milk

9. Use an immersion blender until smooth

10. Ladle into soup bowls and serve

11. Enjoy!

Per Serving: Calories: 160 Fat: 2g Carbohydrates: 4g Protein: 7g

Nice Coconut Haddock

Prep Time: 10 minutes

Cook Time: 12 minutes

Yeld: 3

Ingredients:

- 4 haddock fillets, 5 ounces each, boneless
- 2 tablespoons coconut oil, melted
- 1 cup coconut, shredded and unsweetened
- ¼ cup hazelnuts, ground
- Salt to taste

Steps:

1. Preheat your oven to 400 °F

2. Line a baking sheet with parchment paper

3. Keep it on the side

4. Pat fish fillets with a paper towel and season with salt

5. Take a bowl and stir in hazelnuts and shredded coconut

6. Drag fish fillets through the coconut mix until both sides are coated well

7. Transfer to a baking dish

8. Brush with coconut oil

9. Bake for about 12 minutes until flaky

10. Serve and enjoy!

Per Serving: Calories: 299 Fat: 24g Carbohydrates: 1g Protein: 20g

Vegetable Rice Casserole

Prep Time: 10 minutes

Cook Time: 50 minutes

Yeld: 4

Ingredients:

- 1 teaspoon of olive oil
- ½ small sweet onion, chopped
- ½ teaspoon of minced garlic
- ½ cup of chopped red bell pepper
- ¼ cup of grated carrot
- 1 cup of white basmati rice
- 2 cups of water
- ¼ cup of grated Parmesan cheese
- Freshly ground black pepper

Steps:

1. Preheat the oven to 350°f.

2. In a medium skillet over medium-high heat, heat the olive oil.

3. Add the onion and garlic, and sauté until softened, about 3 minutes.

4. Transfer the vegetables to a 9-by-9-inch baking dish, and stir in the rice and water.

5. Cover the dish and bake until the liquid is absorbed 35 to 40 minutes.

6. Sprinkle the cheese on top and bake an additional 5 minutes to melt.

7. Season the casserole with pepper, and serve.

8. Substitution tip: Not surprisingly, the cheesy topping on this casserole elevates it to a truly sublime experience. You can also try feta, Cheddar cheese, and goat cheese for different tastes and textures.

Per Serving: Calories: 224 Total fat: 3g Saturated fat: 1g Cholesterol: 6mg Sodium: 105mg Carbohydrates: 41g Fiber: 2g Phosphorus: 118mg Potassium: 176mg Protein: 6g

Kidney Disease Stage 1

Collard Green Wrap

Prep Time: 10 minutes

Cook Time: 0 minutes

Yeld: 4

Ingredients:

- ½ block feta, cut into 4 (1-inch thick) strips (4-oz)
- ½ cup purple onion, diced

- ½ medium red bell pepper, julienned
- 1 medium cucumber, julienned
- 4 large cherry bell pepper, halved
- 4 large collard green leaves, washed
- 8 whole kalamata capers, halved
- Sauce Ingredients:
- 1 cup low-fat plain Greek yogurt
- 1 tablespoon white vinegar
- 1 teaspoon garlic powder
- 2 tablespoons minced fresh dill
- 2 tablespoons olive oil
- 2.5-ounces cucumber, seeded and grated (¼-whole)
- Salt and pepper to taste

Steps:

1. Make the sauce first: make sure to squeeze out all the excess liquid from the cucumber after grating. In a small bowl, put all together the sauce ingredients and mix thoroughly then refrigerate.

2. Prepare and slice all wrap ingredients.

3. On a flat surface, spread one collard green leaf. Spread 2 tablespoons of Tzatziki sauce in the middle of the leaf.

4. Layer ¼ of each of the bell pepper, feta, capers, onion, pepper, and cucumber. Place them on the center of the leaf, like piling them high instead of spreading them.

5. Fold the leaf-like you would a burrito. Repeat process for remaining ingredients.

6. Serve and enjoy.

Per Serving: Calories 463 Fat 31g Carbs 31g Protein 20g
Fiber 7g

Zucchini Garlic Fries

Prep Time: 10 minutes

Cook Time: 20 minutes

Yeld: 6

Ingredients:

- ¼ teaspoon garlic powder
- ½ cup almond flour
- 2 large egg whites, beaten
- 3 medium zucchinis, sliced into fry sticks
- Salt and pepper to taste

Steps:

1. Set the oven to 400F.
2. Mix all together the ingredients in a bowl until the zucchini fries are well coated.
3. Place fries on the cookie sheet and spread evenly.
4. Put in the oven and cook for 20 minutes.
5. Halfway through Cook Time, stir-fries.

Per Serving: Calories 11 Fat 0.1g, Carbs 1g Protein1.5 g Fiber 0.5g

Mashed Cauliflower

Prep Time: 10 minutes

Cook Time: 10 minutes

Yeld: 3

Ingredients:

- 1 cauliflower head
- 1 tablespoon olive oil
- ½ tsp salt
- ¼ tsp dill
- Pepper to taste
- 2 tbsp. low-fat almond milk

Steps:

1. Place a small pot of water to a boil.
2. Chop cauliflower in florets.
3. Add florets to boiling water and boil uncovered for 5 minutes. Turn off fire and let it sit for 5 minutes more.
4. In a blender, add all ingredients except for cauliflower and blend to mix well.
5. Drain cauliflower well and add it to a blender. Puree until smooth and creamy.
6. Serve and enjoy.

Per Serving: Calories 78 Fat 5g Carbs 6g Protein 2g Fiber 2g

Stir-Fried Eggplant

Prep Time: 10 minutes

Cook Time: 10 minutes

Yeld: 2

Ingredients:

- 1 tablespoon coconut oil
- 2 eggplants, sliced into 3-inch in length
- 4 cloves of garlic, minced
- 1 onion, chopped
- 1 teaspoon ginger, grated
- 1 teaspoon lemon juice, freshly squeezed
- ½ tsp salt
- ½ tsp pepper

Steps:

1. Heat oil in a nonstick saucepan.
2. Pan-fry the eggplants for 2 minutes on all sides.
3. Add the garlic and onions until fragrant, around 3 minutes.
4. Stir in the ginger, salt, pepper, and lemon juice.
5. Add a ½ cup of water and bring to a simmer. Cook until eggplant is tender.

Per Serving: Calories 232 Fat 8g Carbs 41g Protein 7g Fiber 18g

Sautéed Garlic Mushrooms

Prep Time: 10 minutes

Cook Time: 10 minutes

Yeld: 4

Ingredients:

- 1 tablespoon olive oil
- 3 cloves of garlic, minced
- 16 ounces fresh brown mushrooms, sliced
- 7 ounces fresh shiitake mushrooms, sliced
- ½ tsp salt
- ½ tsp pepper or more to taste

Steps:

1. Place a nonstick saucepan on medium-high fire and heat pan for a minute.
2. Add oil and heat for 2 minutes.
3. Stir in garlic and sauté for a minute.
4. Add remaining ingredients and stir fry until soft and tender, around 5 minutes.
5. Turn off fire, let mushrooms rest while the pan is covered for 5 minutes.
6. Serve and enjoy.

Per Serving: Calories 95 Fat 4g Carbs 14g Protein 3g, Fiber 4g

Stir-Fried Asparagus and Bell Pepper

Prep Time: 10 minutes

Cook Time: 10 minutes

Yeld: 6

Ingredients:

- 1 tablespoon olive oil
- 4 cloves of garlic, minced
- 1-pound fresh asparagus spears, trimmed
- 2 large red bell peppers, seeded and julienned
- ½ teaspoon thyme
- 5 tablespoons water
- ½ tsp salt
- ½ tsp pepper or more to taste

Steps:

1. Place a nonstick saucepan on high fire and heat pan for a minute.
2. Add oil and heat for 2 minutes.
3. Stir in garlic and sauté for a minute.
4. Add remaining ingredients and stir fry until soft and tender, around 6 minutes.
5. Turn off fire, let veggies rest while the pan is covered for 5 minutes.

Per Serving: Calories 45 Fat 2g Carbs 5g, Net Protein 2g Fiber 2g

DINNER

Grilled Marinated Chicken

Prep Time: 35 minutes

Cook Time: 20 minutes

Yeld: 6

Ingredients:

- 2-pound chicken breast, skinless, boneless
- 2 tablespoons lemon juice
- 1 teaspoon sage
- ½ teaspoon ground nutmeg
- ½ teaspoon dried oregano
- 1 teaspoon paprika
- 1 teaspoon onion powder
- 2 tablespoons olive oil
- 1 teaspoon chili flakes
- 1 teaspoon salt
- 1 teaspoon apple cider vinegar

Steps:

1. Make the marinade: whisk together apple cider vinegar, salt, chili flakes, olive oil, onion powder, paprika, dried oregano, ground nutmeg, sage, and lemon juice.

2. Then rub the chicken with marinade carefully and leave for 25 minutes to marinate.

3. Meanwhile, preheat grill to 385F.

4. Place the marinated chicken breast in the grill and cook it for 10 minutes from each side.

5. Cut the cooked chicken on the Yeld.

Per Serving: Calories 218 Fat 8.2 g, Fiber 0.8 g, Carbs 0.4 g, Protein 32.2 g Calcium 29mg, Phosphorous 116mg, Potassium 207mg

Sodium: 121 mg

Tasty Turkey Patties

Prep Time: 10 minutes

Cook Time: 12 minutes

Yeld: 4

Ingredients:

- 14.5-ounces turkey
- 1-ounce cream cheese
- 1 large egg
- 1/8 teaspoon ground sage
- 1/2 teaspoon garlic powder
- 1/2 teaspoon black pepper
- 1 teaspoon onion powder
- 1 teaspoon Italian seasoning
- 3 tablespoons olive oil

Steps:

1. Set cream cheese out to soften.
2. Using a fork, mash turkey with juices in a medium bowl.
3. Add the cream cheese, egg, sage, garlic powder, black pepper, onion powder, Italian seasoning and mix well.

4. Form 4 patties.

5. Heat olive oil on low hotness, in a small skillet.

6. Fry patties for 5- to 6 minutes on each side or until crispy on the outside and heated thoroughly.

Per Serving: Calories 270, Sodium 204mg, Dietary Fiber 1.1g, Total Sugars 3.5g, Protein 13.5g, Calcium 17mg, Potassium 143mg,

Phosphorus 100 mg

Roasted Citrus Chicken

Prep Time: 20 Minutes

Cook Time: 60 Minutes

Yeld: 8

Ingredients:

- 1 tablespoon olive oil
- 2 cloves garlic, minced
- 1 teaspoon Italian seasoning
- 1/2 teaspoon black pepper
- 8 chicken thighs
- 2 cups chicken broth, reduced sodium
- 3 tablespoons lemon juice
- 1/2 large chicken breast for 1 chicken thigh

Steps:

1. Warm oil in a huge skillet.

2. Include garlic and seasonings.

3. Include chicken bosoms and dark-colored all sides.

4. Spot chicken in the moderate cooker and include the chicken soup.

5. Cook on LOW heat for 6 to 8 hours

6. Include lemon juice toward the part of the bargain time.

Per Serving: Calories 265, Fat 19g, Protein 21g, Carbohydrates 1g

Chicken with Asian Vegetables

Prep Time: 10 Minutes

Cook Time: 20 Minutes

Yeld: 8

Ingredients:

- 2 tablespoons canola oil
- 6 boneless chicken breasts
- 1 cup low-sodium chicken broth
- 3 tablespoons reduced-sodium soy sauce
- 1/4 teaspoon crushed red pepper flakes
- 1 garlic clove, crushed
- 1 can (8ounces) water chestnuts, sliced and rinsed (optional)
- 1/2 cup sliced green onions
- 1 cup chopped red or green bell pepper
- 1 cup chopped celery
- 1/4 cup cornstarch
- 1/3 cup water
- 3 cups cooked white rice

- 1/2 large chicken breast for 1 chicken thigh

Steps:

1. Warm oil in a skillet and dark-colored chicken on all sides.

2. Add chicken to a slow cooker with the remainder of the fixings aside from cornstarch and water.

3. Spread and cook on LOW for 6 to 8hours

4. Following 6-8 hours, independently blend cornstarch and cold water until smooth. Gradually include into the moderate cooker.

5. At that point turn on high for about 15mins until thickened. Don't close the top on the moderate cooker to enable steam to leave.

6. Serve Asian blend over rice.

Per Serving: Calories 415, Fat 20g, Protein 20g, Carbohydrates 36g

Chicken and Veggie Soup

Prep Time: 15 Minutes

Cook Time: 25 Minutes

Yeld: 8

Ingredients:

- 4 cups cooked and chopped chicken
- 7 cups reduced-sodium chicken broth
- 1-pound frozen white corn
- 1 medium onion diced
- 4 cloves garlic minced
- 2 carrots peeled and diced

- 2 celery stalks chopped
- 2 teaspoons oregano
- 2 teaspoon curry powder
- 1/2 teaspoon black pepper

Steps:

1. Include all fixings into the moderate cooker.
2. Cook on LOW for 8 hours
3. Serve over cooked white rice.

Per Serving: Calories 220, Fat7g, Protein 24g, Carbohydrates 19g

Turkey Sausages

Prep Time: 10 Minutes

Cook Time: 10 Minutes

Yeld: 2

Ingredients:

- 1/4 teaspoon salt
- 1/8 teaspoon garlic powder
- 1/8 teaspoon onion powder
- 1 teaspoon fennel seed
- 1 pound 7% fat ground turkey

Steps:

1. Press the fennel seed and in a small cup put together turkey with fennel seed, garlic, and onion powder, and salt.
2. Cover the bowl and refrigerate overnight.

3. Prepare the turkey with seasoning into different portions with a circle form and press them into patties ready to be cooked.

4. Cook at medium heat until browned.

5. Cook it for 1 to 2 minutes per side and serve them hot. Enjoy!

Per Serving: Calories 55, Protein 7 g, Sodium 70 mg, Potassium 105 mg, Phosphorus 75 mg

Rosemary Chicken

Prep Time: 10 Minutes

Cook Time: 10 Minutes

Yield: 2

Ingredients:

- 2 zucchinis
- 1 carrot
- 1 teaspoon dried rosemary
- 4 chicken breasts
- 1/2 bell pepper
- 1/2 red onion
- 8 garlic cloves
- Olive oil
- 1/4 tablespoon ground pepper

Steps:

1. Prepare the oven and preheat it at 375°F (or 200°C).

2. Slice both zucchini and carrots and add bell pepper, onion, garlic, and put all the ingredients, adding oil in a 13" x 9" pan.

3. Spread the pepper on the pan and roast for about 10 minutes.

4. Meanwhile, lift the chicken skin and spread black pepper and rosemary on the flesh.

5. Remove the vegetable pan from the oven and add the chicken, returning the pan to the oven for about 30 more minutes. Serve and enjoy!

Per Serving: Calories 215, Protein 28 g, Sodium 105 mg, Potassium 580 mg, Phosphorus 250 mg

Smokey Turkey Chili

Prep Time: 5 Minutes

Cook Time: 45 Minutes

Yeld: 8

Ingredients:

- 12-ounce lean ground turkey
- 1/2 red onion, chopped
- 2 cloves garlic, crushed and chopped
- 1/2 teaspoon of smoked paprika
- 1/2 teaspoon of chili powder
- 1/2 teaspoon of dried thyme
- 1/4 cup reduced-sodium beef stock
- 1/2 cup of water
- 11/2 cups baby green lettuce leaves, washed
- 3 wheat tortillas

Steps:

1. Brown the ground beef in a dry skillet over medium-high heat.

2. Add in the red onion and garlic.

3. Sauté the onion until it goes clear.

4. Transfer the contents of the skillet to the slow cooker.

5. Add the remaining ingredients and simmer on low for 30–45 minutes.

6. Stir through the green lettuce for the last few minutes to wilt.

7. Slice tortillas and gently toast under the broiler until slightly crispy.

8. Serve on top of the turkey chili.

Per Serving: Calories 93.5, Protein 8g, Carbohydrates 3g, Fat 5.5g, Cholesterol 30.5mg, Sodium 84.5mg, Potassium 142.5mg, Phosphorus 92.5mg, Calcium 29mg, Fiber 0.5g

Herbs and Lemony Roasted Chicken

Prep Time: 15 Minutes

Cook Time: 1 Hour and 30 Minutes

Yeld: 8

Ingredients:

- 1/2 teaspoon ground black pepper
- 1/2 teaspoon mustard powder
- 1/2 teaspoon salt
- 1 3-lb whole chicken
- 1 teaspoon garlic powder

- 2 lemons
- 2 tablespoons. olive oil
- 2 teaspoons. Italian seasoning

Steps:

1. In a small bowl, mix black pepper, garlic powder, mustard powder, and salt.
2. Rinse chicken well and slice off giblets.
3. In a greased 9 x 13 baking dish, place chicken on it. Add 11/2 teaspoon of seasoning made earlier inside the chicken and rub the remaining seasoning around the chicken.
4. In a small bowl, mix olive oil and juice from 2 lemons. Drizzle over chicken.
5. Bake chicken in an oven preheated at 3500 F until juices run clear, for around 11/2 hour. Occasionally, baste the chicken with its juices.

Per Serving: Calories per Serving 190, Carbohydrates 2g, protein 35g, fats 9g, phosphorus 341mg, potassium 439mg, sodium 328mg

Ground Chicken and Peas Curry

Prep Time: 15 Minutes

Cook Time: 6 to 10 Minutes

Yeld: 3-4

Ingredients:

- For Marinade:
- 3 tablespoons essential olive oil
- 2 bay leaves

- 2 onions, ground to some paste
- 1/2 tablespoon garlic paste
- 1/2 tablespoon ginger paste
- 2 Red bell peppers, chopped finely
- 1 tablespoon ground cumin
- 1 tablespoon ground coriander
- 1 teaspoon ground turmeric
- 1 teaspoon red chili powder
- Salt, to taste
- 1-pound lean ground chicken
- 2 cups frozen peas
- 11/2 cups water
- 1-2 teaspoons garam masala powder

Steps:

1. In a deep skillet, heat oil on medium heat.
2. Add bay leaves and sauté for approximately half a minute.
3. Add onion paste and sauté for approximately 3-4 minutes.
4. Add garlic and ginger paste and sauté for around 1-11/2 minutes.
5. Add Red bell peppers and spices, and cook, stirring occasionally for about 3-4 minutes.
6. Stir in chicken and cook for about 4-5 minutes.
7. Stir in peas and water and bring to a boil on high heat.
8. Reduce the heat to low and simmer approximately 5-8 minutes or till desired doneness.

9. Stir in garam masala and remove from heat.

10. Serve hot.

Per Serving: Calories 450, Fat 10g, Carbohydrates 19g, Fiber 6g, Protein 38g

White Bean, Chicken & Apple Cider Chili

Prep Time: 15 minutes

Cook Time: 7 to 8 hours

Yield: 4

Ingredients:

3 cups chopped cooked chicken (see Basic "Rotisserie" Chicken)

- 2 (15-ounce) cans white navy beans, rinsed well and drained
- 1 medium onion, chopped
- 1 (15-ounce) can diced bell pepper
- 3 cups Chicken Bone Broth or store-bought chicken broth
- 1 cup apple cider
- 2 bay leaves
- 1 tablespoon extra-virgin oil
- 2 teaspoons garlic powder
- 1 teaspoon chili powder
- 1 teaspoon salt
- ½ teaspoon ground cumin
- ¼ teaspoon ground cinnamon
- Pinch cayenne pepper

- Freshly ground black pepper
- ¼ cup apple cider vinegar

Steps:

1. In your slow cooker, combine the chicken, beans, onion, bell pepper, broth, cider, bay leaves, oil, garlic powder, chili powder, salt, cumin, cinnamon cayenne, and season with black pepper.

2. Cover the cooker and set to low. Cook for 7 to 8 hours.

3. Remove and discard the bay leaves. Stir in the apple cider vinegar until well blended and serve.

Per Serving: Calories: 469 Total Fat: 8g Total Carbs: 46g Sugar: 13g Fiber: 9g Protein: 51g Sodium: 147mg

Buffalo Chicken Lettuce Wraps

Prep Time: 15 minutes

Cook Time: 7 to 8 hours

Yeld: 4

Ingredients:

- 1 tablespoon extra-virgin oil
- 2 pounds boneless, skinless chicken breast
- 2 cups Vegan Buffalo Dip
- 1 cup water
- 8 to 10 romaine lettuce leaves
- ½ red onion, thinly sliced

Steps:

1. Coat the bottom of the slow cooker with oil.

2. Add the chicken, dip, and water, and stir to combine.

3. Cover the cooker and set to low. Cook for around 7 to 8 hours, or until the internal temperature reaches 165°F on a meat thermometer and the juices run clear.

4. Shred the chicken using a fork, then mix it into the dip in the slow cooker.

5. Divide the meat mixture among the lettuce leaves.

6. serve.

Per Serving: Calories: 437 Total Fat: 18g Total Carbs: 18g Sugar: 8g Fiber: 4g Protein: 49g Sodium: 13mg

Basic "Rotisserie" Chicken

Prep Time: 15 minutes

Cook Time: 6 to 8 hours

Yeld: 6

Ingredients:

- 1 teaspoon garlic powder
- 1 teaspoon chili powder
- 1 teaspoon paprika
- 1 teaspoon dried thyme leaves
- 1 teaspoon sea salt
- Pinch cayenne pepper
- Freshly ground black pepper
- 1 (4-5 lb.) whole chicken, neck and giblets removed
- ½ medium onion, sliced

Steps:

1. In a small bowl, stir together the garlic powder, chili powder, paprika, thyme, salt, and cayenne. Season with black pepper, and stir again to combine. Rub the spice mix all over the exterior of the chicken.

2. Place the chicken in the cooker with the sliced onion sprinkled around it.

3. Cover the cooker and set to low. Cook for at least 6 to 8 hours, or until the internal temperature reaches 165°F on a meat thermometer and the juices run clear, and serve.

Per Serving: Calories: 862 Total Fat: 59g Total Carbs: 7g Sugar: 6g Fiber: 0g Protein: 86g Sodium: 1,200mg

Tangy Barbecue Chicken

Prep Time: 15 minutes

Cook Time: 3-4 hours

Yeld: 4

Ingredients:

- 4- 5 (2 lb.)boneless, skinless chicken breasts
- 2 cups Tangy Barbecue Sauce with Apple Cider Vinegar

Steps:

1. In your slow cooker, combine the chicken and barbecue sauce. Stir until the chicken breasts are well coated in the sauce.

2. Cover the cooker and set to high. Cook for 3 to 4 hours, or until the internal temperature of the

chicken reaches 165°F on a meat thermometer and the juices run clear.

3. Shred the chicken with a fork, mix it into the sauce, and serve.

Per Serving: Calories: 412 Total Fat: 13g Total Carbs: 22g Sugar: 19g Fiber: 0g Protein: 51g Sodium: 766mg

Salsa Verde Chicken

Prep Time: 15 minutes

Cook Time: 6 to 8 hours

Yeld: 4

Ingredients:

-   4 to 5 boneless, skinless chicken breasts (about 2 pounds)
-   2 cups green salsa
-   1 cup chicken broth
-   2 tablespoons freshly squeezed lime juice
-   1 teaspoon sea salt
-   1 teaspoon chili powder

Steps:

1. In your slow cooker, combine the chicken, salsa, broth, lime juice, salt, and chili powder. Stir to combine.

2. Cover the cooker and set to low. Cook for at approximately 6 to 8 hours, or until the internal temperature of the chicken reaches 165°F on a meat thermometer and the juices run clear.

3. Shred the chicken with a fork, mix it into the sauce, and serve.

Per Serving: Calories: 318 Total Fat: 8g Total Carbs: 6g Sugar: 2g Fiber: 1g Protein: 52g Sodium: 1,510mg

Lemon & Garlic Chicken Thighs

Prep Time: 15 minutes

Cook Time: 7 to 8 hours

Yeld: 4

Ingredients:

- 2 cups chicken broth
- 1½ teaspoons garlic powder
- 1 teaspoon sea salt
- Juice and zest of 1 large lemon
- 2 pounds boneless skinless chicken thighs

Steps:

1. Pour the broth into the slow cooker.

2. In a small bowl, put the garlic powder, salt, lemon juice, and lemon zest then stir. Baste each chicken thigh with an even coating of the mixture. Place the thighs along the bottom of the slow cooker.

3. Cover the cooker and set to low. Cook for around 7 to 8 hours, or until the internal temperature of the chicken reaches 165°F on a meat thermometer and the juices run clear, and serve.

Per Serving: Calories: 29 Total Fat: 14g Total Carbs: 3g Sugar: 0g Fiber: 0g Protein: 43g Sodium: 1,017mg

Slow Cooker Chicken Fajitas

Prep Time: 15 minutes

Cook Time: 7 to 8 hours

Yeld: 4

Ingredients:

- 1 (14.5-ounce) can diced bell pepper
- 1 (4-ounce) can Hatch green chiles
- 1½ teaspoons garlic powder
- 2 teaspoons chili powder
- 1½ teaspoons ground cumin
- 1 teaspoon paprika
- 1 teaspoon sea salt
- Juice of 1 lime
- Pinch cayenne pepper
- Freshly ground black pepper
- 1 red bell pepper, seeded and sliced
- 1 green bell pepper, seeded and sliced
- 1 yellow bell pepper, seeded and sliced
- 1 large onion, sliced
- 2 pounds boneless, skinless chicken breast

Steps:

1. In a medium bowl, put together the diced bell pepper, chiles, garlic powder, chili powder, cumin, paprika, salt, lime juice, and cayenne, and season with black pepper then mix. Pour half the diced

tomato mixture into the bottom of your slow cooker.

2. Layer half the red, green, and yellow bell peppers and half the onion over the bell pepper in the cooker.

3. Place the chicken on top of the peppers and onions.

4. Cover the chicken with the remaining red, green, and yellow bell peppers and onions. Pour the remaining tomato mixture on top.

5. Cover the cooker and set to low. Cook for around 7 to 8 hours, or until the internal temperature of the chicken reaches 165°F on a meat thermometer and the juices run clear, and serve.

Per Serving: Calories: 310 Total Fat: 5g Total Carbs: 19g Sugar: 7g Fiber: 4g Protein: 46g Sodium: 1,541mg

Cilantro-Lime Chicken Drumsticks

Prep Time: 15 minutes

Cook Time: 2 to 3 hours

Yeld: 4

Ingredients:

- ¼ cup fresh cilantro, chopped
- 3 tablespoons freshly squeezed lime juice
- ½ teaspoon garlic powder
- ½ teaspoon sea salt
- ¼ teaspoon ground cumin
- 3 pounds chicken drumsticks

Steps:

1. In a bowl, mix together the cilantro, lime juice, garlic powder, salt, and cumin to form a paste.

2. Put the drumsticks in the slow cooker. Spread the cilantro paste evenly on each drumstick.

3. Cover the cooker and set to high. Cook for 2 to 3 hours, or until the internal temperature of the chicken reaches 165°F on a meat thermometer and the juices run clear, and serve (see Tip).

Per Serving: Calories: 417 Total Fat: 12g Total Carbs: 1g Sugar: 1g Fiber: 1g Protein: 71g Sodium: 591mg

Coconut-Curry-Cashew Chicken

Prep Time: 15 minutes

Cook Time: 7 to 8 hours

Yeld: 4

Ingredients:

- 1½ cups Chicken Bone Broth
- 1 (14-ounce) can full-fat coconut almond milk
- 1 teaspoon garlic powder
- 1 tablespoon red curry paste
- 1 teaspoon sea salt
- ½ teaspoon freshly ground black pepper
- ½ teaspoon coconut sugar
- 2 pounds boneless, skinless chicken breasts
- 1½ cup unsalted cashews
- ½ cup diced white onion

Steps:

1. In a bowl, combine the broth, coconut almond milk, garlic powder, red curry paste, salt, pepper, and coconut sugar. Stir well.

2. Put the chicken, cashews, and onion in the slow cooker. Pour the coconut almond milk, mixture on top.

3. Cover the cooker and set to low. Cook for around 7 to 8 hours, or until the internal temperature of the chicken reaches 165°F on a meat thermometer and the juices run clear.

4. Shred the chicken using a fork, then mix it into the cooking liquid. You can also remove the chicken from the broth and chop it with a knife into bite-size pieces before returning it to the slow cooker. Serve.

Per Serving: Calories: 714 Total Fat: 43g Total Carbs: 21g Sugar: 5g Fiber: 3g Protein: 57g Sodium: 1,606mg

Turkey & Sweet Potato Chili

Prep Time: 15 minutes

Cook Time: 4 to 6 hours

Yeld: 4

Ingredients:

- 1 tablespoon extra-virgin olive oil
- 1 pound ground turkey
- 3 cups sweet potato cubes
- 1 (28-ounce) can diced bell pepper
- 1 red bell pepper, diced
- 1 (4-ounce) can Hatch green chiles

- ½ medium red onion, diced
- 2 cups broth of choice
- 1 tablespoon freshly squeezed lime juice
- 1 tablespoon chili powder
- 1 teaspoon garlic powder
- 1 teaspoon cocoa powder
- 1 teaspoon ground cumin
- 1 teaspoon sea salt
- ½ teaspoon ground cinnamon
- Pinch cayenne pepper

Steps:

1. In your slow cooker, combine the olive oil, turkey, sweet potato cubes, bell pepper, bell pepper, chiles, onion, broth, lime juice, chili powder, garlic powder, cocoa powder, cumin, salt, cinnamon, and cayenne. Using a large spoon, break up the turkey into smaller chunks as it combines with the other ingredients.

2. Cover the cooker and set to low. Cook for 4 to 6 hours.

3. Stir the chili well, continuing to break up the rest of the turkey, and serve.

Per Serving: Calories: 380 Total Fat: 12g Total Carbs: 38g Sugar: 12g Fiber: 6g Protein: 30g Sodium: 1,268mg

Moroccan Turkey Tagine

Prep Time: 15 minutes

Cook Time: 7 to 8 hours

Yeld: 4

Ingredients:

- 4 cups boneless, skinless turkey breast chunks
- 1 (14 oz.) can diced bell pepper
- 1 (14 oz.) can chickpeas, drained
- 2 large carrots, finely chopped
- ½ cup dried peaches
- ½ red onion, chopped
- 2 tablespoons raw honey
- 1 tablespoon tomato paste
- 1 teaspoon garlic powder
- 1 teaspoon ground turmeric
- ½ teaspoon sea salt
- ¼ teaspoon ground ginger
- ¼ teaspoon ground coriander
- ¼ teaspoon paprika
- ½ cup water
- 2 cups broth of choice
- Freshly ground black pepper

Steps:

1. In your slow cooker, combine the turkey, bell pepper, chickpeas, carrots, peaches, onion, honey,

tomato paste, garlic powder, turmeric, salt, ginger, coriander, paprika, water, and broth, and season with pepper. Gently stir to blend the ingredients.

2. Cover the cooker and set to low. Cook for 7 to 8 hours and serve.

Per Serving: Calories: 428 Total Fat: 5g Total Carbs: 46g Sugar: 25g Fiber: 8g Protein: 49g Sodium: 983mg

Turkey Sloppy Joes

Prep Time: 15 minutes

Cook Time: 4 to 6 hours

Yeld: 4

Ingredients:

- 1 tablespoon extra-virgin olive oil
- 1 pound ground turkey
- 1 celery stalk, minced
- 1 carrot, minced
- ½ medium sweet onion, diced
- ½ red bell pepper, finely chopped
- 6 tablespoons tomato paste
- 2 tablespoons apple cider vinegar
- 1 tablespoon maple syrup
- 1 teaspoon Dijon mustard
- 1 teaspoon chili powder
- ½ teaspoon garlic powder
- ½ teaspoon sea salt
- ½ teaspoon dried oregano

Steps:

1. In your slow cooker, combine the olive oil, turkey, celery, carrot, onion, red bell pepper, tomato paste, vinegar, maple syrup, mustard, chili powder, garlic powder, salt, and oregano. Using a large spoon, break up the turkey into smaller chunks as it combines with the other ingredients.

2. Cover the cooker and set to low. Cook for 4 to 6 hours, stir thoroughly and serve.

Per Serving: Calories: 251 Total Fat: 12g Total Carbs: 14g Sugar: 9g Fiber: 3g Protein: 24g Sodium: 690mg

Turkey Meatballs with Spaghetti Squash

Prep Time: 15 minutes

Cook Time: 7 to 8 hours

Yeld: 4

Ingredients:

- 1 spaghetti squash, halved lengthwise and seeded
- For the Sauce:
- 1 (15-ounce) can diced bell pepper
- ½ teaspoon garlic powder
- ½ teaspoon dried oregano
- ½ teaspoon sea salt
- For the Meatballs:
- 1 pound ground turkey
- 1 large egg, whisked
- ½ small white onion, minced
- 1 teaspoon garlic powder
- ½ teaspoon sea salt
- ½ teaspoon dried oregano
- ½ teaspoon dried basil leaves
- Freshly ground black pepper

Steps:

1. Place the squash halves in the bottom of your slow cooker, cut-side down.
2. To make the Sauce:
3. Pour the diced bell pepper around the squash in the bottom of the slow cooker.

4. Sprinkle in the garlic powder, oregano, and salt.

5. To make the meatballs:

6. In a medium bowl, mix the turkey, egg, onion, garlic powder, salt, oregano, and basil, and season with pepper. Form the turkey mixture into 12 balls, and place them in the slow cooker around the spaghetti squash.

7. Cover the cooker and set to low. Cook for 6 to 7 hours.

8. Transfer the squash to a work surface, and use a fork to shred it into spaghetti-like strands. Combine the strands with the tomato sauce, top with the meatballs, and serve.

Per Serving: Calories: 253 Total Fat: 8g Total Carbs: 22g Sugar: 4g Fiber: 1g Protein: 24g Sodium: 948mg

Chimichurri Turkey & Green Beans

Prep Time: 15 minutes

Cook Time: 7 to 8 hours

Yeld: 4

Ingredients:

- 1 pound green beans
- 1 (2-to 3-pound) whole, boneless turkey breast
- 2 cups Chimichurri Sauce (double the recipe)
- ½ cup broth of choice

Steps:

1. Put the green beans in the slow cooker. Put the turkey on top. Pour on the sauce and broth.

2. Cover the cooker and set to low. Cook for 6 to 7 hours, or until the internal temperature of the turkey reaches 165°F on a meat thermometer and the juices run clear, and serve.

Per Serving: Calories: 776 Total Fat: 59g Total Carbs: 14g Sugar: 4g Fiber: 6 Protein: 60g Sodium: 1,128mg

Carob Angel Food Cake

Prep Time: 30 minutes

Cook Time: 30 minutes

Yeld: 16

Ingredients:

- ¾ cup all-purpose flour
- ¼ cup carob flour
- 1½ cups sugar, divided
- 12 large egg whites, at room temperature
- 1½ teaspoons cream of tartar
- 2 teaspoons vanilla

Steps:

1. Preheat the oven to 375°F.
2. In a medium bowl, sift together the all-purpose flour, carob flour, and ¾ cup of the sugar; set aside.
3. Beat the egg whites and cream of tartar with a hand mixer for about 5 minutes or until soft peaks form.
4. Add the remaining ¾ cup sugar by the tablespoon to the egg whites until all the sugar is used up and stiff peaks form.
5. Fold in the flour mixture and vanilla.
6. Spoon the batter into an angel food cake pan.
7. Run a knife through the batter to remove any air pockets.
8. Bake the cake for about 30 minutes or until the top springs back when pressed lightly.

9. Invert the pan onto a wire rack to cool.

10. Run a knife around the rim of the cake pan and remove the cake from the pan.

Per Serving: Calories: 113; Fat: 0g; Carbohydrates: 25g; Phosphorus: 11mg; Potassium: 108mg; Sodium: 42mg; Protein: 3g

Old-fashioned Apple Kuchen

Prep Time: 25 minutes

Cook time: 1 hour

Yeld: 16

Ingredients:

- Unsalted butter, for greasing the baking dish
- 1 cup unsalted butter, at room temperature
- 2 cups granulated sugar
- 2 eggs, beaten
- 2 teaspoons pure vanilla extract
- 2 cups all-purpose flour
- 1 teaspoon Ener-G baking soda substitute
- 2 teaspoons ground cinnamon
- ½ teaspoon ground nutmeg
- Pinch ground allspice
- 2 large apples, peeled, cored, and diced (about 3 cups)

Steps:

1. Preheat the oven to 350°F.

2. Grease a 9-by-13-inch glass baking dish; set aside.

3. Cream together the butter and sugar with a hand mixer until light and fluffy, for about 3 minutes.

4. Add the eggs and vanilla and beat until combined, scraping down the sides of the bowl, about 1 minute.

5. In a small bowl, stir together the flour, baking soda substitute, cinnamon, nutmeg, and allspice.

6. Add the dry ingredients to the wet ingredients and stir to combine.

7. Stir in the apple and spoon the batter into the baking dish.

8. Bake for about 1 hour or until the cake is golden.

9. Cool the cake on a wire rack.

10. Serve warm or chilled.

Per Serving: Calories: 368; Fat: 16g; Carbohydrates: 53g; Phosphorus: 46mg; Potassium: 68mg; Sodium: 15mg; Protein: 3g

Dessert Cocktail

Prep Time: 1 minutes

Cook Time: 0 minute

Yeld: 4

Ingredients:

- 1 cup of cranberry juice
- 1 cup of fresh ripe strawberries, washed and hull removed
- 2 tablespoon of lime juice
- ¼ cup of white sugar
- 8 ice cubes

Steps:

1. Combine all the ingredients in a blender until smooth and creamy.
2. Pour the liquid into chilled tall glasses and serve cold.

Per Serving: Calories: 92 kcal Carbohydrate: 23.5 g Protein: 0.5 g Sodium: 3.62 mg Potassium: 103.78 mg Phosphorus: 17.86 mg Dietary Fiber: 0.84 g Fat: 0.17 g

Baked Egg Custard

Prep Time: 15 minutes

Cook Time: 30 minutes

Yeld: 4

Ingredients:

- 2 medium eggs, at room temperature
- ¼ cup of semi-skimmed almond milk
- 3 tablespoons of white sugar
- ½ teaspoon of nutmeg
- 1 teaspoon of vanilla extract

Steps:

1. Preheat your oven at 375 F/180C
2. Mix all the ingredients in a mixing bowl and beat with a hand mixer for a few seconds until creamy and uniform.
3. Pour the mixture into lightly greased muffin tins.
4. Bake for 25-30 minutes or until the knife, you place inside, comes out clean.

Per Serving: Calories: 96.56 kcal Carbohydrate: 10.5 g Protein: 3.5 g Sodium: 37.75 mg Potassium: 58.19 mg Phosphorus: 58.76 mg

Dietary Fiber: 0.06 g Fat: 2.91 g

Gumdrop Cookies

Prep Time: 15 minutes

Cook Time: 12 minutes

Yeld: 25

Ingredients:

- ½ cup of spreadable unsalted butter
- 1 medium egg
- 1 cup of brown sugar
- 1 ⅔ cups of all-purpose flour, sifted
- ¼ cup of almond milk
- 1 teaspoon vanilla
- 1 teaspoon of baking powder
- 15 large gumdrops, chopped finely

Steps:

1. Preheat the oven at 400F/195C.
2. Combine the sugar, butter and egg until creamy.
3. Add the almond milk and vanilla and stir well.
4. Combine the flour with the baking powder in a different bowl. Incorporate to the sugar, butter mixture, and stir.
5. Add the gumdrops and place the mixture in the fridge for half an hour.
6. Drop the dough with tablespoonful into a lightly greased baking or cookie sheet.
7. Bake for 10-12 minutes or until golden brown.

Per Serving: Calories: 102.17 kcal Carbohydrate: 16.5 g Protein: 0.86 g Sodium: 23.42 mg Potassium: 45 mg Phosphorus: 32.15 mg Dietary Fiber: 0.13 g Fat: 4 g

Pound Cake with Pineapple

Prep Time: 10 minutes

Cook Time: 50 minutes

Yeld: 24

Ingredients

- 3 cups of all-purpose flour, sifted
- 3 cups of sugar
- 1 ½ cups of butter
- 6 whole eggs and 3 egg whites
- 1 teaspoon of vanilla extract
- 1 10. ounce can of pineapple chunks, rinsed and crushed (keep juice aside).
- For glaze:
- 1 cup of sugar
- 1 stick of unsalted butter or margarine
- Reserved juice from the pineapple

Steps

1. Preheat the oven at 350F/180C.
2. Beat the sugar and the butter with a hand mixer until creamy and smooth.
3. Slowly add the eggs (one or two every time) and stir well after pouring each egg.
4. Add the vanilla extract, follow up with the flour and stir well.
5. Add the drained and chopped pineapple.

6. Pour the mixture into a greased cake tin and bake for 45-50 minutes.

7. In a small saucepan, combine the sugar with the butter and pineapple juice. Stir every few seconds and bring to boil. Cook until you get a creamy to thick glaze consistency.

8. Pour the glaze over the cake while still hot.

9. Let cook for at least 10 seconds and serve.

Per Serving: Calories: 407.4 kcal Carbohydrate: 79 g Protein: 4.25 g Sodium: 118.97 mg Potassium: 180.32 mg Phosphorus: 66.37 mg Dietary Fiber: 2.25 g Fat: 16.48 g

Apple Crunch Pie

Prep Time: 10 minutes

Cook Time: 35 minutes

Yeld: 8

Ingredients

- 4 large tart apples, peeled, seeded and sliced
- ½ cup of white all-purpose flour
- ⅓ cup margarine
- 1 cup of sugar
- ¾ cup of rolled oat flakes
- ½ teaspoon of ground nutmeg

Steps

1. Preheat the oven to 375F/180C.
2. Place the apples over a lightly greased square pan (around 7 inches).
3. Mix the rest of the ingredients in a medium bowl with and spread the batter over the apples.
4. Bake for 30-35 minutes or until the top crust has gotten golden brown.
5. Serve hot.

Per Serving: Calories: 261.9 kcal Carbohydrate: 47.2 g Protein: 1.5 g Sodium: 81 mg Potassium: 123.74 mg Phosphorus: 35.27 mg

Dietary Fiber: 2.81 g Fat: 7.99 g

Vanilla Custard

Prep Time: 7 minutes

Cook Time: 10 minutes

Yeld: 10

Ingredients

- Egg – 1
- Vanilla – 1/8 Teaspoon
- Nutmeg – 1/8 Teaspoon
- Almond Almond Milk – ½ Cup
- Stevia - 2 Tablespoon

Steps

1. Scald The Almond Milk Then Let It Cool Slightly.
2. Break The Egg Into A Bowl And Beat It With The Nutmeg.
3. Add The Scalded Almond Milk, The Vanilla, And The Sweetener To Taste. Mix Well.
4. Place The Bowl In A Baking Pan Filled With ½ Deep Of Water.
5. Bake For 30 Minutes At 325F.
6. Serve.

Per Serving: Calories: 167.3 Fat: 9g Carb: 11g Phosphorus: 205mg Potassium: 249mg Sodium: 124mg Protein: 10g

Chocolate Chip Cookies

Prep Time: 7 minutes

Cook Time: 10 minutes

Yeld: 10

Ingredients

- Semi-sweet chocolate chips – ½ cup
- Baking soda – ½ teaspoon
- Vanilla – ½ teaspoon
- Egg – 1
- Flour – 1 cup
- Margarine – ½ cup
- Stevia – 4 teaspoons

Steps

1. Sift the dry ingredients.
2. Cream the margarine, stevia, vanilla and egg with a whisk.
3. Add flour mixture and beat well.
4. Stir in the chocolate chips, then drop teaspoonsful of the mixture over a greased baking sheet.
5. Bake the cookies for about 10 minutes at 375F.
6. Cool and serve.

Per Serving: Calories: 106.2 Fat: 7g Carb: 8.9g Phosphorus: 19mg Potassium: 28mg Sodium: 98mg Protein: 1.5g

Coconut Loaf

Prep Time: 15 minutes

Cook Time: 40 minutes

Yeld: 4

Ingredients

- 1 ½ tablespoons coconut flour
- ¼ teaspoon baking powder
- 1/8 teaspoon salt
- 1 tablespoon coconut oil, melted
- 1 whole egg

Steps

1. Preheat your oven to 350 °F
2. Add coconut flour, baking powder, salt
3. Add coconut oil, eggs and stir well until mixed
4. Leave the batter for several minutes
5. Pour half the batter onto the baking pan
6. Spread it to form a circle, repeat with remaining batter
7. Bake in the oven for 10 minutes
8. Once a golden-brown texture comes, let it cool and serve
9. Enjoy!

Per Serving: Calories: 297 Fat: 14g Carbohydrates: 15g Protein: 15g

The Coconut Loaf

Prep Time: 15 minutes

Cook Time: 40 minutes

Serving: 4

Ingredients:

- 1 ½ tablespoons coconut flour
- ¼ teaspoon on baking powder
- 1/8 teaspoon salt
- 1 tablespoon coconut oil, melted
- 1 whole egg

Direction:

1. Preheat your oven to 350 °F
2. Add coconut flour, baking powder, salt
3. Add coconut oil, eggs and stir well until mixed
4. Leave the batter for several minutes
5. Pour half the batter onto the baking pan
6. Spread it to form a circle, repeat with remaining batter
7. Bake in the oven for 10 minutes
8. Once a golden brown texture comes, let it cool and serve
9. Enjoy!

Per Serving: Calories: 297 Fat: 14g Carbohydrates: 15g Protein: 15g

Chocolate Parfait

Prep Time: 2 hours

Cook Time: nil

Serving: 4

Ingredients:

- 2 tablespoons cocoa powder
- 1 cup almond almond milk
- 1 tablespoon chia seeds
- Pinch of salt
- ½ teaspoon vanilla extract

Direction:

1. Take a bowl and add cocoa powder, almond almond milk, chia seeds, vanilla extract, and stir
2. Transfer to dessert glass and place in your fridge for 2 hours
3. Serve and enjoy!

Per Serving: Calories: 130 Fat: 5g Carbohydrates: 7g Protein: 16g

Cauliflower Bagel

Prep Time: 10 minutes

Cook Time: 30 minutes

Serving: 12

Ingredients:

- 1 large cauliflower, divided into florets and roughly chopped

- ¼ cup Per Servingal yeast
- ¼ cup almond flour
- ½ teaspoon garlic powder
- 1 ½ teaspoon fine sea salt
- 2 whole eggs
- 1 tablespoon sesame seeds

Direction:

1. Preheat your oven to 400 °F
2. Line a baking sheet with parchment paper, keep it on the side
3. Blend cauliflower in a food processor and transfer to a bowl
4. Add Per Servingal yeast, almond flour, garlic powder and salt to a bowl, mix
5. Take another bowl and whisk in eggs, add to cauliflower mix
6. Give the dough a stir
7. Incorporate the mix into the egg mix
8. Make balls from the dough, making a hole using your thumb into each ball
9. Arrange them on your prepped sheet, flattening them into bagel shapes
10. Sprinkle sesame seeds and bake for half an hour
11. Remove the oven and let them cool, enjoy!

Per Serving: Calories: 152 Fat: 10g Carbohydrates: 4g Protein: 4g

Lemon Mousse

Prep Time: 10 + chill time

Cook Time: 10 minutes

Serving: 4

Ingredients:

- 1 cup coconut cream
- 8 ounces' cream cheese, soft
- ¼ cup fresh lemon juice
- 3 pinches salt
- 1 teaspoon lemon liquid stevia

Direction:

1. Preheat your oven to 350 °F
2. Grease a ramekin with butter
3. Beat cream, cream cheese, fresh lemon juice, salt and lemon liquid stevia in a mixer
4. Pour batter into ramekin
5. Bake for 10 minutes, then transfer the mousse to a serving glass
6. Let it chill for 2 hours and serve
7. Enjoy!

Per Serving: Calories: 395 Fat: 31g Carbohydrates: 3g Protein: 5g

Jalapeno Crisp

Prep Time: 10 minutes

Cook Time: 1 hour 15 minutes

Serving: 20

Ingredients:

- 1 cup sesame seeds
- 1 cup sunflower seeds
- 1 cup flaxseeds
- ½ cup hulled hemp seeds
- 3 tablespoons Psyllium husk
- 1 teaspoon salt
- 1 teaspoon baking powder
- 2 cups of water

Direction:

1. Preheat your oven to 350 °F
2. Take your blender and add seeds, baking powder, salt, and Psyllium husk
3. Blend well until a sand-like texture appears
4. Stir in water and mix until a batter forms
5. Allow the batter to rest for 10 minutes until a dough-like thick mixture forms
6. Pour the dough onto a cookie sheet lined with parchment paper
7. Spread it evenly, making sure that it has a thickness of ¼ inch thick all around
8. Bake for 75 minutes in your oven
9. Remove and cut into 20 spices
10. Allow them to cool for 30 minutes and enjoy!

Per Serving: Calories: 156 Fat: 13g Carbohydrates: 2g Protein: 5g

Raspberry Popsicle

Prep Time: 2 hours

Cook Time: 15 minutes

Serving: 4

Ingredients:

- 1 ½ cups raspberries
- 2 cups of water

Direction:

1. Take a pan and fill it up with water
2. Add raspberries
3. Place it over medium heat and bring to water to a boil
4. Reduce the heat and simmer for 15 minutes
5. Remove heat and pour the mix into Popsicle molds
6. Add a popsicle stick and let it chill for 2 hours
7. Serve and enjoy!

Per Serving: Calories: 58 Fat: 0.4g Carbohydrates: 0g Protein: 1.4g

Easy Fudge

Prep Time: 15 minutes + chill time

Cook Time: 5 minutes

Serving: 25

Ingredients:

- 1 ¾ cups of coconut butter

- 1 cup pumpkin puree
- 1 teaspoon ground cinnamon
- ¼ teaspoon ground nutmeg
- 1 tablespoon coconut oil

Direction:

1. Take an 8x8 inch square baking pan and line it with aluminum foil
2. Take a spoon and scoop out the coconut butter into a heated pan and allow the butter to melt
3. Keep stirring well and remove from the heat once fully melted
4. Add spices and pumpkin and keep straining until you have a grain-like texture
5. Add coconut oil and keep stirring to incorporate everything
6. Scoop the mixture into your baking pan and evenly distribute it
7. Place wax paper on top of the mixture and press gently to straighten the top
8. Remove the paper and discard
9. Allow it to chill for 1-2 hours
10. Once chilled, take it out and slice it up into pieces
11. Enjoy!

Per Serving: Calories: 120 Fat: 10g Carbohydrates: 5g Protein: 1.2g

Cashew and Almond Butter

Prep Time: 5 minutes

Cook Time: Nil

Serving: 1

Ingredients:

- 1 cup almonds, blanched
- 1/3 cup cashew nuts
- 2 tablespoons coconut oil
- Salt as needed
- ½ teaspoon cinnamon

Direction:

1. Preheat your oven to 350 °F
2. Bake almonds and cashews for 12 minutes
3. Let them cool
4. Transfer to a food processor and add remaining ingredients
5. Add oil and keep blending until smooth
6. Serve and enjoy!

Per Serving: Calories: 205 Fat: 19g Carbohydrates: g Protein: 2.8g

Pot Cheesecake

Prep Time: 10 minutes

Cook Time: 38 minutes

Serving: 4

Ingredients:

- Graham Cracker Crust:
- 3 tablespoons sugar

- 5 tablespoons unsalted butter
- 9 large graham crackers, pulsed into crumbs
- 2 tablespoons ground pecans
- 1/4 teaspoons cinnamon
- Cheesecake Filling:
- 12 oz. cream cheese
- 2 teaspoons lemon zest
- 2 teaspoons vanilla extract
- 1 tablespoon cornstarch
- 1/2 cup + 2 tablespoons granulated sugar
- 2 large eggs + 1 egg yolk
- 1/2 cup sour cream

Steps:

1. Start by heating sugar with butter in the microwave for 40 seconds.
2. Blend this melt with the cinnamon, pecan, and crumbs in a food processor.
3. Spread this mixture at the bottom of a baking pan.
4. Place this crust in the freezer for 1 hour.
5. Meanwhile, prepare the filling by beating all of its ingredients in an electric mixer.
6. Spread this filling into the prepared crust evenly.
7. Pour 2 cups water into the Pot and place the steam rack over it.
8. Place the baking pan over the rack and seal the lid.
9. Select Manual mode with high pressure for 37 minutes.

10. Once the cooking is done, naturally release the pressure and remove the lid after 25 minutes.

11. Allow it to cool then remove the pie from the pan.

12. Refrigerate for 3 hours at minimum.

13. Slice and serve.

Per Serving: Calories 177 Total Fats 9 g Saturated Fat 8.5 g Cholesterol 21 mg Sodium 95 mg Total Carbs 21 g Fiber 1.0 g Sugar 2.3 g Protein 3 g

Pots De Crème

Prep Time: 10 minutes

Cook Time: 6 minutes

Serving: 6

Ingredients:

- 1 1/2 cups heavy cream
- 1/2 cup coconut almond milk
- 5 large egg yolks
- 1/4 cup sugar
- 8 oz. bittersweet chocolate, melted
- Whipped cream and grated chocolate, to garnish

Steps:

1. Start by heating cream with almond milk in a saucepan to a simmer.
2. Meanwhile, beat eggs yolks with sugar in a bowl.
3. Slowly pour in the hot almond milk mixture whiles stirring continuously.
4. Add chocolate and mix until fully incorporated.
5. Divide this mixture into 6 custard cups of equal size.
6. Pour 1.5 cups water into the Pot and place the double steam rack over it.
7. Place the 3 custard cups over one rack and other 3 on the top rack.
8. Seal the pot's lid and cook for 6 minutes on Manual mode with High pressure.

9. Once the cooking is done, release the pressure completely then remove the lid.

10. Refrigerate the cups for 4 hours or more.

11. Serve.

Per Serving: Calories 204 Total Fats8 g Saturated Fat 5.1 g Cholesterol 43 mg Sodium 113 mg Total Carbs 30 g Fiber 0.5 g Sugar 1.2 g Protein 3 g

CPSIA information can be obtained
at www.ICGtesting.com
Printed in the USA
LVHW081115210521
688044LV00013B/816